To Stewart
from Margaret and Jack
Christmas, 1990

DUNDEE
CITY OF DISCOVERY

LORN
MACINTYRE

PETER
ADAMSON

Acknowledgements

For help with obscure queries, Lorn Macintyre is grateful for the courtesy and patience of: the staff of the Local History Room, Central Library, Wellgate Centre, Dundee; and Mr Kenneth Fraser, the Library, University of St Andrews.

First published in 1988 by
Alvie Publications
52 Buchanan Gardens
St. Andrews KY16 9LX

ISBN 0 9511 800

Printed by Allen Litho Ltd., Kirkcaldy

Monochrome and colour separations,
Hislop and Day Ltd. Edinburgh.

Page make-up, Andrew M. Mackie.

Photypeset by University of St. Andrews Printing Department.

FOREWORD BY
THE LORD PROVOST OF DUNDEE

Since 1986, RRS *Discovery*, Captain Scott's ship of Antarctic fame, has resided in Dundee.

A special dock is being prepared with a connecting Heritage Centre and *Discovery* is to become the focal point of a £30m shopping and leisure development along the Waterfront, part of Dundee's splendid river frontage.

The city is now using the theme, Dundee, City of Discovery, and we are literally telling the world about the benefits of working and living in Dundee.

As well as trying to attract new industry to the city, I should like to see Dundee become a main tourist centre. We have so much to offer with excellent recreational and leisure facilities which have been greatly enhanced in recent years by the addition of three new flumes at the Leisure Centre, and the construction of three other sports centres. In addition we can offer golf, fishing, hill walking and a great deal more, all on our doorstep.

Also in Dundee we have many beautiful parks and open spaces which are used to provide much needed leisure facilities for local residents and tourists. Indeed the surroundings at Camperdown Country Park are the envy of many people who visit Dundee.

In recent weeks we have seen the opening of the new City Square. This is a marvellous new facility for the city, and the District Council is proud to have provided such an amenity for the people of Dundee. Now the city is the proud possessor of a fine new centre-piece. This new-look Square is definitely for the people — totally for the use of pedestrians, with the fountains, floral displays and floodlights highlighting the surrounding buildings. It will undoubtedly prove most attractive to our citizens and tourists.

I must congratulate Lorn Macintyre and Peter Adamson on this book with its excellent black and white and colour photographs which will give readers some impressions of Dundee and will, I hope, provide Dundonians with an incentive to learn more about their city and encourage others to come and "Discover" Dundee. I can assure you that a very warm welcome awaits.

Thomas Mitchell

As the trains rumbled across the new Tay bridge in 1878 travellers to Dundee noticed the big excavations between the railway and the firth. The reason why so many important looking men were getting their boots dirty was a heap of shells. Material was needed for an embankment to extend the harbour, but work had stopped because the shovels had just uncovered a colossal "kitchen-midden". It showed, it was claimed, that the little fishing village of the Stannergait had been one of the first settlements.

It seems that around 6500 BC these prototype Dundonians squatted by the estuary, devouring a diet of edible molluscs while they contemplated the development of such a splendid site. How come that the midden, twelve feet under the soil, also contained porpoise-bones as well as stone implements?

These primitive people exploited the fertile soil of the Carse of Gowrie, where ploughs still turn up stone that hacked at forests. Weapons hacked at people when desirable territory was coveted. The Law was a natural place on which to construct a defensive fort.

History is a many-layered affair. Those excavators of 1878 discovered a dozen cists or coffins interred eight feet above the shell bed, probably from Roman times. It must have been an awesome sight for first century AD watchers on the Law, seeing the Roman armies heading for their marching camps near Longforgan and Murroes.

The Romans left corpses behind, but they also left glass-making skills and new ways of cultivating the land. The Roman invasion turned the tribes into collective opposition called the Caledonii, and so the concept of Scotland was born.

It's maddening how little we know about the Picts who occupied Scotland north of the Forth till the ninth century when the charismatic Kenneth McAlpin, king of the Scots, took over their kingdom. But maybe the symbols the Picts incised on stones at places like Strathmartine will one day become clear to us when we have need of their knowledge, for they seem to have been magicians of sorts.

King William the Lion acknowledged Dundee's status when he granted it its first charter as a Royal burgh towards the end of the twelfth century. Legend avers that the king's brother, David, Earl of Huntingdon, having survived the Crusades, disembarked at Dundee and showed his thanks for deliverance from the infidels by founding a church dedicated to St Mary, the city's patron saint. Is this why a seal of the city dated 1416 was inscribed: *Dei Donum* — God's Gift?

Despite the lilies and the blue field on Dundee's coat of arms in reverence of St Mary, the story has not been a peaceful one. Embroiled in the Scottish Wars of Independence, the Tay town was laid waste in 1303 by Edward the First, the "Hammer of the Scots". Dundee Castle was taken, and the churches the citizens were sheltering in were put to the torch.

Wallace's head became a macabre warning set above London Bridge, but in 1306 Bruce was crowned at Scone. Three years later the Great Council of the Clergy of Scotland, gathering in the Greyfriars' Monastery in Dundee blessed Bruce as the true king of the Scots.

Dundee was laid siege to in 1311, and held so obstinately by William de Montfichet the governor that a treaty was concluded to give it up within a stipulated time. But Edward the Second ordered the governor on pain of death to hold fast. Edward Bruce, the Scottish king's brother, launched an impetuous attack and succeeded in capturing the town. But after the triumph of Bannockburn in 1314, Bruce went to stay in Dundee to show his thanks.

George Wishart defied the plague and an assassination attempt to preach to Dundonians as the "Geneva of the North" eagerly embraced the Reformation. It was an important town, a bustling centre of the wool and linen industries, its Nine Trades Craft Guilds flourishing, its busy harbour putting it second only to Edinburgh. The rich merchants went about their business in their French clothes, and their wives tugged their cloaks round them against the chill of the Tay as their shoes avoided the mire.

Dundonians minded their manners and kept their prejudices to themselves. That devout Catholic Mary Queen of Scots was courteously received several times. But the renewal of the Solemn League and Covenant by Scotland was to be disastrous for Dundee. James, Earl of Montrose was an enthusiast for the Covenant and then its sworn enemy. On the morning of 4th April 1645 as the clocks on steeples amd mantelpieces were striking ten the Great Marquis arrived in Dundee.

Instead of surrendering, the insulted townsfolk threw Montrose's trumpeter into prison. Maddened, he ordered the storming of Dundee. But the soldiers were too busy filling their pockets to spread the fire of their torches. It was worse when General Monck appeared at the gates of the town at the end of July 1651.

Tragically, Dundonians had got into the habit of breakfasting in the alehouses. One contemporary writer was scathing: "the tounsemen did no dewtey in their awn deffence, but wer most of them all drunken, lyke so maney beasts." Monck struck on 1st September: Almost 800 of the garrison and citizens were slaughtered. The gold, silver and jewellery they looted made soldiers rich men for life.

Then there were the alleged enemies within. In 1669 prosecutions for witchcraft were revived with barbaric enthusiasm. Poor Grizzel Jaffray, spouse of James Butchard, maltman, and prisoner in the Tolbooth had to answer "the horrid crime of witchcraft," and *in extremis* accused other persons of being practitioners of the black arts. It is said that while she was being executed in the Seagate, her only son sailed into the port as captain of his own vessel, after a long absence. On being told that it was his mother who was the cause of all the bustle, he turned his ship round and never returned to Dundee.

Was there to be no end to destruction and death in the Tayside town? John Graham of Claverhouse, created Viscount Dundee for his services to the crown, brought more than shame on the place from which he had taken his title when he set Hilltown ablaze in 1689.

It was the last hostile attack made on Dundee, though the town dallied with the Old Pretender in the Jacobite rising of 1715. In 1745 Dundonians were on the other side and, having celebrated the victory of Culloden, gave the freedom of Dundee to the Duke of Cumberland.

It would seem that the citizens were tired of strife. William Adam's new Town House of 1734 was a symbol of prosperity and stability. The flax and linen industries were flourishing, with less dependence on the Dighty Burn. It has been estimated that between 1815 and 1830, at least £250,000 had been spent improving the harbour. Between 1816 and 1833 Dundee's population had expanded from 30,000 to 50,000. By 1833 the Earl Grey Dock was being constructed. Everything was ready for the arrival of jute, whose story is told elsewhere in this book.

Meantime let this other boat bring in its cargo, wives cheering on the wharf. Albatrosses accompanied this ship till they saw the harpoon shot, the whale that would never harm a man thrashing in the polar sea, then being hauled aboard to be flensed, cut up to remove the blubber. Its oil is the precious commodity.

Since the late eighteenth century and probably before that, whalers had been putting out from Dundee, first under spreading sails, then by steam propulsion. They hunted seals off Greenland in the spring, and harried whales off Canada in the summer, and sometimes the ice put pressure on them. The quest for the world's largest mammal kept the hammers going in the shipyards of Tayside. By 1872 Dundee was Britain's leading whaling port. But as the end of the century approached, whaling ceased to be viable, with the natural oil no longer needed in the jute industry.

In 1892 Queen Victoria granted Dundee a Royal Charter. The ancient burgh became a city, which it had been for ages, and the Chief Magistrate was to be addressed as Lord Provost. Dundee appeared to be a prosperous city, with ladies sitting in the sun, listening to the harmony from the Magdalen Green bandstand while their sisters sweated in the mills, which the owners refused to invest in for the future.

The idle, undernourished thirties were followed by the privations of war, with 11,000 mothers and children evacuated early on from the city. The Caledon shipyard built warships, maintaining and repairing submarines.

After 1945 new light engineering firms were attracted to the new industrial estates. The opening of the Tay Road Bridge in 1966 caused the demolition of the Royal Arch of 1844, but it brought new prosperity to the city. The rest of this book follows the success story of Dundee to the present, to the multi-million pound Waterfront Development that may uncover another "kitchen-midden," showing how far the City of Discovery has come.

In December 1879 at the height of a ferocious storm the first Tay railway bridge collapsed while a north-bound train was crossing. Seventy five travellers including children, lost their lives. But Dundonians are not brooders. In 1887 the new bridge was opened. In September 1987 its centenary was celebrated by a brilliant display of pyrotechnic concoctions (10,500 principal explosions) from a crossing north-bound train and a moored boat in the calm evening. It was also the promotion of Dundee as the City of Discovery, and 200,000 turned out to watch. There were few complaints about the tail-back from the other bridge afterwards.

These youngsters may be about to audition for Jack and the Beanstalk. Dundee's 60 year old Dramatic Society is one of the most successful companies in the country, with its own Little Theatre in Victoria Road, the triumphant conversion of a jute store. The Repertory Theatre, which seats 450, has outstanding acoustics as well as style thanks to sympathetic local architects. It also mounts art exhibitions. The Rep encourages the young ones to express themselves: its Youth and Community Heritage Project allows 50 Dundee and Tayside teenagers to take over the running of the theatre for several weeks in the summer. If it's musicals you yearn for, the Whitehall (the former Alhambra Music Hall) is your venue. Film buffs should make for the Steps Theatre in the Wellgate complex.

The make-up of artistic enterprise: Dundee College of Further Education
has developed a one year Theatre Arts preparatory course, designed
mainly for students going on to drama college, and community drama
projects. Sheila Allan is the inspiration behind this innovation, which,
as Theatre in Education, tours primary schools in Tayside. As this
picture was being taken, "A Scottish Tale" by Marilyn Paton, one of the
students, was about to go out on the road.

If you meet her in the early morning, make way for her. Liz Lynch is a Dundee lass in a hurry who has been running and training almost daily since she was eleven. Her winged feet have taken her across the ocean, to study sports management and recreation at the University of Alabama. Who can forget her victory in the 10,000 metres at the Commonwealth Games, Edinburgh? 1987 was a hectic year. She shattered the British and Commonwealth records for the 10,000 metres in the World Championship final in Rome in September. The following month she found the time to stand still at the altar beside the northern Ireland steeplechase runner Peter McColgan. Liz is now helping her native city keep fast and fit through her post as athletics development officer with the District Council.

Opposite, hundreds turn out for the Dundee People's Marathon, 1988.

Buildings as well as seasons change. In Lochee Road, the sculptured pediment of Tay Carpet Works (1865) gave a functional building distinction. But the bulldozers didn't get yet another casuality of the textile slump. Now snooker balls click instead of spindles. Part of it has been converted into students' flats in this age of equal opportunity.

Veeder-Root are always speeding ahead of the times, making tachographs and petrol pumps in Dundee. The products of this 40 year old business go all over the world. They have to think ahead: if the price of petrol goes up, a little adjustment to the pump gets the right amount out of you.

Dundee Ice Rink was opened fifty years ago and offers curling, skating and ice hockey at its Kingsway West complex. Its newest star, keeping a sense of balance despite so much success, is 16 year old Fiona Ritchie. Fiona was British Junior Figure-Skating Champion in 1986 and 1987, and bronze medallist in the Senior Championship in both years. She was also Scottish Senior Champion in 1987, and has competed in the World Junior Championship in Canada and Australia.

EDUCATION

St Andrews is the oldest university in Scotland, but Dundee has its own identity, its own institution. The idea of a university for Dundee was first proposed in the middle of last century, but no funding was available. Local philanthropy came to the fore in the form of the Baxter family, ever generous in putting something back into the city that had made their fortune. Miss Mary Baxter gave £120,000, and with her relative Dr John Boyd Baxter she signed a deed of foundation declaring that the aim of the new college was to promote "the education of both sexes and the study of science, literature and fine arts."

In 1883 University College was inaugurated, but the early years were ones of financial struggle. In 1897 the College was affiliated to St Andrews University, but relations were strained. In the nineteen fifties the College was given a new name, Queen's College, along with a new constitution, which helped its sense of individual pride. But the call for independence was not heeded till 1967, when the University of Dundee was given its charter, becoming a university in its own right, distinct from St Andrews. HM the Queen Mother was its first Chancellor.

With its faculties of Medicine and Dentistry, Science, Law, Engineering and Applied Science, Arts and Social Sciences and Environmental Studies, Dundee University can compete with any similar institution in the land. The Law faculty's authority in Oil and Gas Law shows the practical contribution the University has made in terms of the economy of the UK through North Sea exploration. Likewise with the academic-based sciences in the prosperous development of the city itself.

In recent years the severe cut-backs in university funding have weakened the university and brought calls for a "remarriage" with St Andrews University. Whereas sensible economics indicate closer "trans-Tay" co-operation and ties with Stirling University, the majority opinion is that reintegration is both unlikely and undesirable.

Though expansion has meant local prosperity, there has been some inevitable loss of character, with the eighteenth century row that housed the university at the end of last century having to be demolished in the nineteen sixties, since space was needed for new buildings. The stylish University Tower, opened in 1961, was the first tower block to be built in the centre of Dundee.

Dundee is well served by institutions of further education. Founded in 1906 as Dundee Training College, the College of Education moved in 1920 from Small's Wynd to its own building in Park Place. In 1975 it moved to the new college in West Ferry. In 1987 it amalgamated with Aberdeen College of Education, becoming the Northern College of Education. Primary teachers are trained on the Dundee campus, secondary in Aberdeen.

There has been more reorganisation in education. In 1985 Dundee College of Commerce and Kingsway Technical College amalgamated to become Dundee College of Further Education. The College is spread over half a dozen sites and offers an astonishing range of courses for those seeking new opportunities. At the commanding hillside site close to the Royal Infirmary subjects such as retail distribution and computing can be studied. The former Technical College site will train those with different touches, from building trades to hairdressing. The close contacts between the College of Further Education and local industry and commerce ensure that the area's needs are being met. The same can be said for the College of Technology.

The artistic can learn to express themselves by attending Duncan of Jordanstone College of Art, founded as a School of Art in 1892 as part of the Technical Institute. The college now occupies buildings in the Perth Road. Degree courses are offered in Fine Art, Design, Interior Design and Architecture, Town Planning and Visual Communications. The book-binder and the weaver can also learn there on part-time courses.

Dundee has distinguished secondary schools. But when the Burgh School Board came into being in 1873 it had no schools to administer, since the Grammar School, the Academy and the English School had been brought together under one roof as Dundee Public Seminaries (now the High School) which were administered by directors. But the Board was about to take over the Seminaries, which were in financial trouble, when ex Baillie William Harris offered £10,000 so that the Board could build its own school for advanced teaching.

The new-style Harris Academy which was to provide both elementary and advanced education for reasonable fees was opened in 1885, with a rector and fifteen assistants supposed to minister to 1035 pupils. Even from the early days it was obvious that the accommodation could not cope with demand.

The next project was Morgan Academy, named after John Morgan, a Dundonian who made his fortune in India. But his will, for the benefit of his native city, was disputed in the courts. The town won the case, and the Morgan Hospital was built. The model was Heriot's Hospital, Edinburgh, and the Dundee establishment was "for the education, lodging, boarding, and clothing of 100 boys, the sons of tradesmen, mechanics, and persons of the working class generally, whose parents stand in need of assistance, to enable them to educate their families who are orphans in need of such assistance."

Morgan Hospital was opened on Craigie estate in 1868. Though it had some of the dark aspects of a Victorian institution, there was some educational enlightenment: "the more degrading kinds of corporal punishment shall be avoided or resorted to as seldom as possible and never for mere literary deficiency if unaccompanied with moral blame."

The School Board bought the Hospital buildings and opened them as a day school in 1889, with 650 pupils and fifteen teachers. The funds of the Trust were applied to the payment of fees of foundationers and to the provision of bursaries for attendance at evening classes in higher or technical education. It is now a comprehensive school in all senses of that word, and the building with its distinguished Gothic features is elevated both in its site and the quality of its education.

Dundee University's Arts Tower and Library of 1961 is an elegant
contribution to the skyline.

A portrait of the mature university: Dundee's Geddes Quadrangle (1909).

Does the name Dundee come from *Dun Deagh* or *Daigh*, the vitrified Iron age fort on the Law? The lazy and less able can drive up this 571 foot volcanic boss, but it presented no problem to these two youngsters. The object between them is not an obsolete factory chimney about to topple into the estuary, but the road bridge. Across the water, Newport-on-Tay and beyond, Tentsmuir Forest on the way to St Andrews.

A new perspective on the familiar: on the summit of the Law, the massive memorial to the sacrifices of two world wars.

The Caird Hall, a jute baron's imposing gift

BROUGHTY FERRY

On a summer afternoon in Dundee East station the merchant prince in his wing collar sits in the carriage, watching the young ones in their blue sailor suits coming on with long-skirted mothers and nannies. They are all bound for Broughty Ferry, the merchant prince to his splendid house built on jute on the hill, the young ones to the beach. Now isn't it a pity that these urchins on the platform can't come because, he thinks, they look in need of a good wash.

But they don't have the sixpence for the bathers' return ticket because their mothers, who work in the merchant prince's mill, can't spare it. (The merchant prince will go home to a hot bath run by a servant). But don't be too hard on the gentleman in the wing collar: he does use some of his profits for public good.

The merchant prince frowns and takes his watch from his waistcoat. But they're all aboard and the whistle goes, the steam train hurrying them along the shore of the estuary.

Before the railway arrived in 1848 Broughty Ferry was a cluster of fisherfolks' cottages round the harbour of Partan Craig (crab rock), and a square keep. Broughty Castle was completed by Andrew, Lord Gray, around 1496. The English occupied it in 1547, and consolidated their situation by building a fort on Balgillo Hill. But three years later it was recovered. Protestants and Catholics then brawled over it. It was offered for sale in 1821 with the suggestion that it would make "an excellent situation for an inn."

In 1861 Sir Rowand Anderson reconstructed it for the War Office as a strategic point to control the Tay. But there were no invasions (apart from the folk of Dundee and further afield wanting a dip) and it was used as a coastguard station. It became a railway storage place, and the lines of bathing-boxes began to lengthen on the beach.

In the old gazetteers, Dundee and Broughty Ferry are four miles apart, but they have been getting closer and closer, with more and more building pushing out the boundaries of both places. Yet, though Broughty was incorporated with Dundee in 1913, it has preserved its own identity, a grid-system of spacious streets laid out as early as 1801 by Charles Hunter of Burnside.

These were the days when there was no Tay rail bridge, when the boats came and went between Broughty and Ferryport-on-Tay, the big paddle ferry carrying wagons, smaller boats carrying the trunks of students going to study at St Andrews, because Dundee still had to get its own university college.

This was "the Brighton of Scotland," and the trains kept steaming in all summer. Our merchant prince can see the lines of bathing-boxes on the sand, and as he goes up the hill to his fine house which looks as if it can hold a dozen families, he frowns to see grandmother hitching up her severe black hem for a paddle with the toddlers down at the beach.

The fisher folk are sitting outside their cottages, the men mending nets, the clay pipes cold in their mouths because there isn't time to stop. Fish don't take holidays. The women are out in the sun too, but their eyes are sore, and so are their fingers, after baiting hundreds of hooks. As for the bare-footed bairns, they are watching these fancy kids on the beach, some of them having to be held so that they can learn to swim. If your father's a fisherman you go in at the deep end.

The bathing-belles in their knee-long costumes have disappeared forever into the swell, but the occasional bikini can still be seen, climate permitting. Don't think that the place has lost its summer zest, however. It's many years since the White Coons sang their swansong on the stand on the beach, but there's still plenty of entertainment. Broughty Ferry Traders, an association of more than 90 businesses, continue the tradition of a Gala Week in July, with attractions for all ages. In the old days there were donkey races; now there's a BMX bicycle event and a beach barbecue.

The history of the Ferry is told graphically in Broughty Castle Museum, its lower floor following the burgh's evolution from one catch to another, fishing to trippers. Dundee's importance as a whaling port is remembered on the second floor, including a model of *Terra Nova,* a Dundee whaler chosen by Captain Scott for his last journey to the Antarctic.

The panorama of the Tay estuary opens up from the museum's observation room. On the vast sand flat between Broughty Ferry and Monifieth curlew call overhead, and shells are treasures.

Naturally Broughty Ferry can boast connections with the famous. (This is not a tall story). A circus elephant died on the road between Broughty Ferry and Dundee in 1706, and was dissected by Patrick Blair, the surgeon apothecary. It was the first such dissection in Britain and must have taken days. Probably the elephant died of a broken heart because it was leaving the Ferry folk.

Now here's a mystery story. Night after night some thirty years ago folk noticed a light at the first floor window of a large house called Winsterly, where a man was bent over a leather-topped desk. The big Bible on a stand on the desk had notes in the margins, but that wasn't what he was working on, though he was a devout supporter of the Church of Christ in Dundee. Dudley D. Watkins was inspired, which was why he was working late. The name means nothing to you? Well, he is said to be the greatest comic artist that Britain has ever produced, and in that Broughty Ferry room night after night he drew Desperate Dan, Lord Snooty, Biffo the Bear, and others in more adventures for D.C. Thomson's comics and papers. Watkins died at that Broughty Ferry desk, but The Broons and Oor Wullie live on for our delight.

As for our merchant prince who came off the train with us in his bowler when a straw hat would have been more appropriate, and, if you please, an umbrella in a heatwave, you won't find his grand house now because, you see, good fortune doesn't last for ever. Mark you, he gave Dundee a park where all those urchins could run about without getting into mischief.

Broughty Castle as the birds see it.

Claypotts is the kind of castle everyone feels they could live in comfortably. But it wasn't built for cosiness. John Strachan erected it between 1560 and 1588 for defensive purposes. "Thieves will need knock ere they durst enter" was one laird's comment on this fortified villa. It is classic z-plan, with diagonally opposite angle towers having gun-loops at ground level. The castle passed to the Grahams of Claverhouse in 1625. In a wonderful state of preservation and administered by Ancient Monuments, Claypotts is essential viewing.

Inclining to a stroll, with Broughty Castle flying the flag. How many such Scottish keeps have had a new lease of life?

This rare survivor, an intact opulent mansion in almost eight acres at Monifieth built by a jute baron, was put on the market recently at offers in excess of £400,000.

This level crossing in the centre of Broughty Ferry comes as a surprise. The railway was a mixed blessing, bringing business but cutting the town in two. This speeding junior has his own form of locomotion.

This is no optical joke on the Broughty Ferry — Monifieth road. You have to go round to the back of the big arch to get the gist: "This gateway and fountain were erected in commemoration of Her Majesty's Jubilee by James Guthrie Orchar Esq Chief Magistrate of Broughty Ferry and were presented by him to the community on 19th September 1887." There isn't a better known name in Broughty. The commemorative arches are at Reres Hill. Orchar intended having a building erected to house his collection of nineteenth century Scottish paintings for the edification of Ferry folk and others. But the endowment he left went towards the purchase of the villa that had belonged to Stephen the shipbuilder, builder of Scott's *Discovery*. But the gallery has been closed, though not without a fight by Ferry folk.

East Church, Broughty Ferry, by Andrew Heiton (1865).

The address is 7 Camphill Road, Broughty Ferry, the lodge of one of the most famous mansions of Dundee's textile tycoons. Carbet Castle was the residence of the Grimond family, from whom the famous Liberal leader is descended. The Grimonds and Gilroys were rivals, their business fortunes and hence status displayed in the grandeur of their homes. Carbet Castle with its many bays was built piecemeal to keep up with the Gothic extravagance of Castleroy, but the latter was the bigger. Both have been demolished, but an 1871 painted ceiling by Charles Frechou (whose most notable work is the Paris Opera House) was saved from Carbet in an ingenious "sandwich" operation. The ceiling is now in safe custody, and, one hopes, will be put on public display eventually.

An old-timer ponders under the clock on the clinic at the corner of Brook Street and Brown Street. Not that he's in any need of attention. But other passers-by couldn't remember what the building had been previously; such is progress.

James and Jennifer Dunlap outside Barometer Cottage, one of the most picturesque dwellings on the waterfront at Broughty Ferry. Jennifer is a local lass, James an American in the oil business with an obvious love for Scotland. The Bell fisher family built this cottage in 1812 and held on to it until 1975. The Meteorological Society installed the barometer in its sentry box for the benefit of the fishermen of Broughty Ferry. On at least two occasions other fishing villages along the coast, with no barometer to warn them to stay at home, suffered drownings. A sign of the times: the instrument was stolen about ten years ago.

Fred Duncan contemplates the eye of the camera. He has looked into the eyes of many fellow Dundonians, but was not an optician. He began as a photographer at the medical school, then went to take a less gory view with Valentines the postcard people. When that company ceased postcard production he returned to medical photography, this time to a study of the eye. Now retired, it pleases him that the pictures he took thirty years ago are still being used to enlighten medical students. His hobby is collecting cameras. He has a Lowden, made in Dundee circa 1880, and a Nimslo, made by Timex in the same city a century later.

Life Drawing Class, Duncan of Jordanstone College.

Dundee is blessed with over 1700 acres of parks and gardens. Over a century ago the Baxter mill dynasty gifted 34 acres, including the large Victorian pavilion designed by Sir Joseph "Crystal Palace" Paxton. But Sir James Caird gave 262 acres in the philanthropic competition to improve the lives and lungs of the citizens. Camperdown Park is certainly the largest, at 735 acres, and probably the most beautiful. Rare trees include the weeping wych-elm, said to be the parent of all weeping elms in the country. The Camperdown Wildlife Centre contains an extensive collection of native and foreign animals, including a brown bear and eagles.

St Ninian's, Methven Street, Lochee, a plain box church of the early
nineteenth century, is close to the gates of Camperdown Works.

D.C. THOMSON

It's easy to see that D.C. Thomson stands for tradition. Adverts are still found on the front page of the Dundee *Courier*, and in the *Sunday Post*, Oor Wullie's as popular as ever.

DCT are an enduring bastion in the precarious world of publishing, where papers fold or are taken over.

It was in the eighteen seventies that William Thomson, a Dundee shipowner, launched himself into publishing by taking shares in a local firm which published the *Dundee Courier and Argus* (founded 1816) and the *Weekly News* (1855).

When William Thomson gained full control in 1886, his son D. C. Thomson became his partner, and over the years nephews were taken on as fully committed partners. There was something of a newspaper war in Dundee between W. and D. C. Thomson and the bigger firm of John Leng & Co. Ltd, publishers of the *Dundee Advertiser* (1801), the *Dundee Evening Telegraph* (1877), the *People's Journal* (1858) and the *People's Friend* (1869).

In 1906 the two businesses came together, with Thomsons as the majority partner, and, inevitably, as owners. In 1926 after the General Strike the *Dundee Advertiser* merged with the *Courier*, which today has the biggest sale of any provincial newspaper in the UK.

Have you ever come across an old paper, the *Post Sunday Special*, in the attic, or under old linoleum? You should have kept it, because it was launched in Glasgow in 1914 and became the *Sunday Post*, which has been in the *Guinness Book of Records* as the "most read newspaper." It seems that seven out of ten of the entire population of Scotland over 15 look forward to it.

D. C. Thomson created great comics. It all began in 1921 with the *Adventure*, a story paper in text form for boys. 1937 is a date so many children should be grateful for. That was the year when the *Dandy* first appeared, and the following year, the *Beano*, which has the largest sale of any comic in the UK.

Thomson knew what their readers wanted, which is why the *Weekly News* sold over a million copies each week. There are *Friendship Books* on shelves throughout the land, and adults still add to the comic annuals they started collecting as children. In fact, early comics in good condition (rare, because you wanted to go back to them again and again while eating a piece on jam) fetch big prices.

Some newspaper owners are acquisitive, but D. C. Thomson have never coveted other people's papers. Their only acquisition was the *Scots Magazine*, which they purchased in 1927 (believe it or not, it was first published in 1739).

Seventeen weekly magazines, five weekly papers and two monthly magazines, plus sixteen twice-weekly library titles add up to the employment of 2900 people in Dundee, London, Glasgow, Manchester and elsewhere, many of whom spend the whole of their working lives at DCT.

This lady is not buying the *Sporting Post* to check her treble-chance, but the odds are that she's taking another Thomson paper, the *Evening Telegraph*.

The gentleman (left) doesn't look too pleased at the presumption of the camera across the street. But at the same corner stance one of the best-kent figures in the city refuses to let the headlines at his feet appear in his face. For half a century Tommy Small gave the news, good and bad, to hurrying Dundonians. He himself made news in the evening paper when he took poorly and had to retire at the age of 69. He'd never had a day's illness, so why bother to register with a doctor?

St Andrew's Church, Cowgait, showed the power of Dundee Trades as
well as the Almighty. It was built over two centuries ago to a design by
Samuel Bell, a wright who became the town's first architect. He was
also responsible for the Trades Hall (demolished) in the High Street.
There were seats for the conveners of the Trades in the front gallery of
St Andrew's, and they worshipped in their gold chains, giving thanks
for their prosperity. Their emblems are commemorated in fine stained
glass windows. Some years ago lightning struck the steeple, but it was
restored.

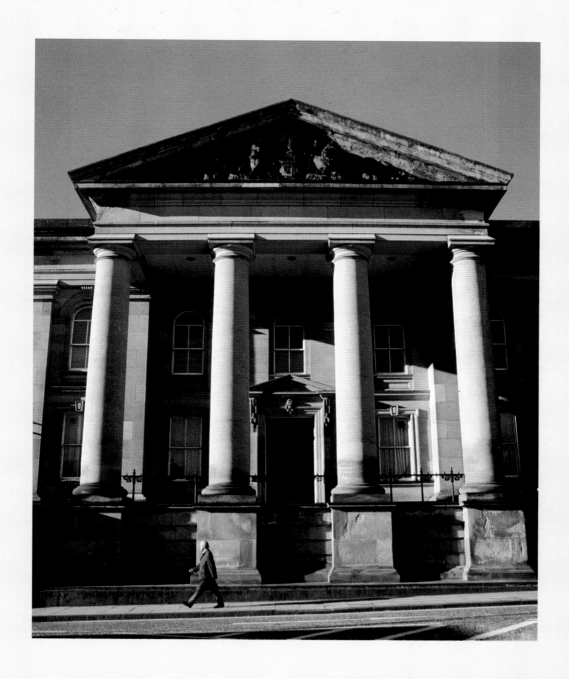

Justice is dispensed from the Sheriff Court, West Bell Street, designed, as a result of a competition, by George Angus in 1833. But it was built by his former pupil William Scott in 1863. Sometimes even the law must give way: much of the west wing was removed to allow the widening of Lochee Road.

Sheriff Edward Bowen presides over stylishly refurbished No I court.

Money used to be dispensed from the Princes Street branch of the Dundee Savings Bank. It comes as a surprise to learn that it dates only from 1914, by David Baxter. The Court will continue to pronounce on the misdemeanours of Dundonians; the bank is undergoing "internal modernisation" to become something else, but the Edwardian Renaissance façade gets a reprieve.

The National Cash Register Company were the first Americans to put their faith in Dundee after the war. By 1969 they were handing out 6,000 pay packets in half a dozen factories round the city. These were the boom times for cash registers, until decimalisation rang the changes, and the work-force was reduced drastically. Nevertheless, NCR have adapted to these electronic times, and supply banks and buildings with computer equipment. The automated telling machine you tap for cash outside your bank may well be an NCR product.

A father and sons made distinguished contributions to the architecture of Dundee. James Thomson became City Architect in 1904 and City Engineer in 1906. His visionary plans anticipated the traffic volume on the Kingsway by-pass, and he wanted the docks infilled as well as the provision of new municipal buildings. But Sir James Caird's £100,000 hand-out for a city hall in 1914 became a headache for Thomson. The jute philanthropist was against a grand design, but the plans had to be amended due to the last-minute gift of a colonnade, delaying the completion of the Caird Hall until 1922. Thomson's son Frank found creative peace in his London digs to produce his brilliant Renaissance Blackness Library in 1904. Another son Harry designed Craigie, a garden suburb for the workers, in 1919. It is called keeping Dundee in the family.

At the corner of Albert Street and Craigie Street, Mr Thrifty minds his own business in the tenement's last stand. The dog seems very tied up.

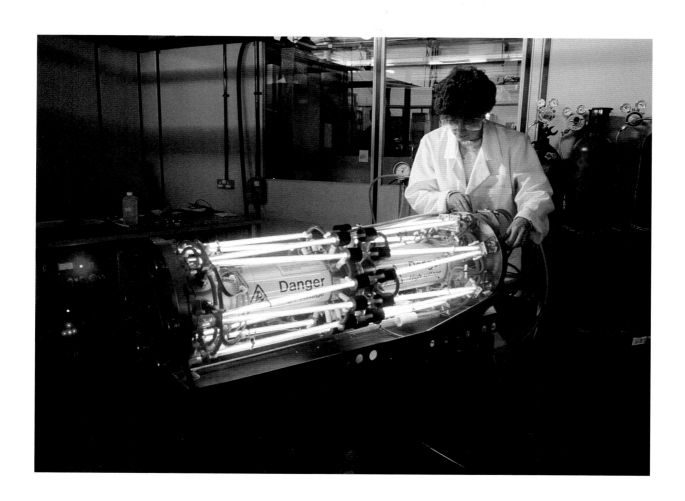

After 35 years in Dundee, Ferranti know all about the glow of success. They make lasers from 1 watt to 10,000 watts of output power for use in scientific, industrial, medical and military processes, which means worldwide. They were the first company in Europe to make gas lasers in 1963, and are now the largest manufacturers of carbon dioxide lasers in the UK. The picture shows an MF series laser used primarily for cutting.

From a hillside in Angus this kilted figure looks towards Dundee. Scott Sutherland ARSA made this evocative memorial in 1969, to the honour of the ranks of the 4th and 5th Dundee and Angus battalions of the Black Watch who gave their lives in the Second World War. The statue was resited recently and will always move hearts.

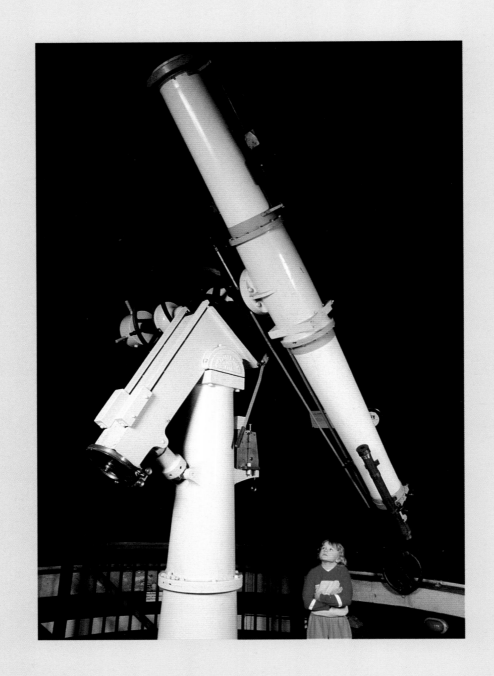

OBSERVING THE HEAVENS FROM BALGAY HILL

The Victorian magnates could be hard taskmasters in their factories, but their philanthropy is another matter. The Baxters and Cairds gave parks for exercise and enjoyment, but John Mills wanted his fellow Dundonians to lift their eyes above the trees.

The linen and twine manufacturer was a member of the Original Secession Kirk, science and religion coming together in perfect focus in his passion for astronomy. Mills built himself a private observatory on the slope of the Law. An old print shows that it had a transit room, proving that he was timing the passage of stars across the meridian and therefore no dilettante.

Mills left his worldly fortune for "the provision of a building equipped with astronomical and other instruments suitable for the study of the wonder and beauty of the works of God in creation." The Mills Observatory has the distinction of being unique in the history of amateur astronomy in Britain "in that it is the only observatory conceived, designed and erected solely for use by the general public."

The Observatory was to be sited on the summit of the Law, but the hostilities of 1914 killed this scheme. In its place a war memorial was erected. It wasn't until the nineteen thirties that the Observatory project was mooted again, since it was felt that its construction could give much-needed work to the depressed building industry. The Astronomer Royal for Scotland chose the Balgay Hill site. It proved an inspired choice, since trees protected the Hill from the glare of the city's lighting, giving a clear atmosphere for viewing.

The Mills Observatory was opened in late 1935, though to some Dundonians it will seem that its dome has been a skyline feature for much longer. A nice consideration of the early days was that visitors could use four-inch Turret telescopes to view the scenery from the balcony.

For the technically minded, the original telescope given by the Mills Trust was an 18 inch Newtonian reflector, electrically driven. The hand-operated dome is made of paper-mache on a steel framework, and most of it has withstood the weather of the past half century. Who remembers that the park gates used to be locked at dusk, which meant that children had to be accompanied by adults, in case they were shut in for the night? When the railings were removed during the war that access problem was solved.

The Newtonian reflector was replaced by a 10-inch Cooke refracting telescope from St Andrews University, particularly suited for fine lunar and planetary detail. In July 1969, during the period of the first Apollo landing, the Observatory had the biggest crowd in its history, when a colour TV and lectures kept the audience moon-struck. In June 1984 Dr Patrick Moore, the television stargazer, opened the new improved facilities of the Mills Observatory. Young and old are welcome to come and take a look.

The little burn of Lochee drove Dundee's destiny and wove the legend. It was one Cox who saw the potential of the running water when he arrived in the district around 1700. By the end of that century several hundred handlooms were busy making money for David Cox.

The jute industry grew out of the linen or flax spinning and weaving trade. Dundee had a stable flax industry in the late eighteenth century, and was central to the coarse linen trade of that region, supplying clothing for America's negro slaves.

Raw jute is the fibre from plant barks. Experiments with it began cautiously on Tayside in the eighteen thirties, but another ingredient was to be necessary for Dundee's renown. The whalers brought back barrels of oil, and at Ruthven Mill, William Taylor experimented with batching — softening the fibre with a mixture of oil and water. Jute yarn production is taken to date from 1833 at the Chapelshade Works, the site now occupied by Dundee College of Technology.

The Cox Brothers virtually created Lochee through the establishment of their Camperdown Works, spread over 30 acres and with a payroll of around 6,000. The population of Lochee increased fourfold between 1841-51. Tents and soldiers' clothing were needed in the Crimean War (1854-56). In the American Civil War (1861-65), jute and linen were in massive demand because cotton wasn't available from the southern states. With the opening up of Australia in the eighteen fifties, British immigrants were crying out for temporary jute canvas houses.

One commentator on the mid nineteenth century has observed: "At the height of the boom any man who could buy or rent a tumbledown mill could make a fortune." Cox Brothers weren't content with Lochee multiplying the family fortune. In 1862 they became shipowners, and the following year established their own jute presses near Calcutta. But competition in spinning and weaving was growing in India, and in 1872 the *Advertiser* had cautioned: "King Jute is a mighty monarch ... but are we sure that the monarch will reign for ever?"

Though the Franco-Prussian War (1870-73) helped Dundee, the Victorian boom was over. But jute was still a big employer. In 1895 43,360 souls, the majority of them women and young ones, were employed in the mills in and around Dundee, with 392,025 tons of jute being landed on Tayside that same year. But by 1905 there were 21,195 power looms in Calcutta, as against 13,704 in the UK.

Mill work was sweated labour, the abundance of old photographs showing the dangerous working conditions among the machines and unguarded pulleys. It made girls into weary women going home to tenements to cook for families. The contradictory paternalism of the mill owners gave the workers public parks, but few hours in which to enjoy the freedom and fresh air.

It seems sad that the spasmodic prosperity of Dundee's jute industry should have been based on wars. In 1915 the city's mills were said to be producing one million sandbags a day for the government. But this wartime boom had been for coarse goods, and after 1918 prices and demand tumbled. Mills began to close. There were 41,220 employed in the industry in 1924; that fell to 27,980 by 1938. New machinery that needed skilled male operators put thousands of women out of the mills. Another sign of depression was an import surplus in 1937 when previously there had been high exports.

A Second World War brought big orders for sandbags, but it weakened the industry further by taking vital male labour away from the mills. Peace brought more international blows, with the partitioning of the Indian subcontinent into the independent states of India and Pakistan restricting British supplies of both raw jute and finished jute goods.

Jute Control had been established in 1939 and continued in the post-war years as a means of protecting the home market from Indian competition. In 1946 a Board of Trade committee recommended the protection of the Dundee mills from the competition from Calcutta. Re-equipment and reorganisation seemed the best hopes for survival, and between 1945 and 1951 an estimated £4 million was laid out.

Prices of imported jute goods were adjusted through Control to protect Dundee's producers from India's industrious mills. The city had an advantage over the subcontinent in yarn for woven carpets and backing cloth for linoleum. But in the mid fifties the linoleum market began its decline, and only the emergence of the tufted carpet industry saved the day in Dundee and elsewhere, since the carpet backing could be woven on jute looms used in the production of linoleum backing.

But technological advances do not bring comfort and security for everyone. Dundee's busy looms slowed with the development of polypropylene, a man-made fibre that could be woven into a cloth. As carpet backing and container material it captured the market from jute. Another cruel blow was that the new, swifter polypropylene weaving looms required fewer operators.

It looked like disaster for Dundee. In the period 1945-77 the number of firms in the traditional jute industry contracted from 37 to 14. By 1962 the number of workers in the jute trade was down to 14,000. But in resilient Dundee, survival spells diversification. Some firms produced jute goods that did not compete with the Calcutta mills. Others also kept faith with their workforce, adapting their plants to the manufacture of polypropylene and other man-made fibres. Some textile firms have been increasing their engineering interests through North Sea oil exploration.

This saga of jute began in Lochee where David Cox brought the weavers together and helped to create one of the world's great industries. The colossal Camperdown factory of the dynasty is being demolished, but something else will rise in its place. Lochee has atmosphere, and on a walk through its streets on an evening with a moon over the Law, one feels surrounded by the ghosts of these weary lassies on their way home from the works.

Chimney stacks as well as church steeples are landmarks on the Dundee skyline. Mill building on the grand scale was about more than market confidence, and Camperdown was the largest of them all. Even at night the silhouette of Cox's Stack is unmistakable, though there is no smoke now. This 280 foot campanile chimney was designed by James Maclaren in conjunction with Cox's own drawing office. The mill is being demolished, but the Stack survives. Admire it, but remember all those thousands who sweated to keep it stoked.

The streets around Camperdown Works are quiet now, the Stack a relic of busy days, when jute meant jobs.

It could be the entrance foyer to a block of fashionable Paris apartments. Actually it's the mill building of Upper Dens, an award-winning triumph of conversion. The original factory of Baxter Brothers dates from the eighteen thirties. Its site, on the steep sided valley of the Dens burn, was crucial to trap the water supply. It expanded into the largest flax and linen producing mill in Dundee, employing 4,000 workers by 1864. After 1870 it was developed as a jute mill. It closed in 1978. Five years later the site was acquired by Hillcrest Housing Association. The listed A mill building has been converted into 73 flats, 34 single and 39 two person. A lift takes the residents up to quiet well-lit corridors where machinery once thundered in the gloom. They sleep peacefully where weary mill workers dreamed of rest. The entrance murals are by students from the Duncan of Jordanstone College of Art, and the resources of the Dundee Public Arts Programme have been utilised in the open space. There are other houses on the mill site through the partnership development of three housing associations — Hillcrest, Servite and Gowrie — funded by the Housing Corporation. The Development is the first winner in Scotland of the Royal Town Planning Institute Silver Jubilee award.

This view from a shattered window is one of survival through adaptation, the modern story of Dundee's mills. This mill started as Manhattan Works in 1874, since most of its products went for export to the States. The business was organised under the name F. S. Sandeman & Sons till amalgamation with other manufacturers in the Dundee area made it part of Jute Industries Limited. In 1950 the factory roof had to be raised seven feet to accommodate new circular loom machinery to produce cloth for ten million jute bags a year. Women were still wanted in the mills: Manhattan had a nursery to hold 65 weans while their mothers earned in the mill. Now trading as Sidlaw Yarns, Manhattan the survivor produces quality yarns mainly for carpet manufacturers.

Dundee Docks have been dealing with oil for a long time. Last century whalers brought in oil for processing jute. Now supply boats from Dundee service the North Sea oil platforms. These two supply vessels are temporarily tied up, but will be sailing again soon, now that the tide is turning, and with new oil-fields promising big yields.

MRS. BEGBIE

This is the face of the oldest person in Britain. Mrs Kate Begbie's astonishing 111 year span can be measured by the fact that she was a toddler when the Tay Bridge collapsed in 1879. But she wasn't in the grief-struck city at the time. Aged eight, she and her brother were brought from Shropshire to Kirriemuir by her Dundee mother.

While Mrs Begbie's mother trained as a nurse at the Infirmary, the daughter became one of the first pupils at the Harris Academy (opened 1885) where in her pinafore she would stand round the piano singing long-forgotten songs. The girl was boarded in Balfour Street (demolished) with a music teacher.

She went to school in a Victorian city of smoke pollution and the evening clatter of jute workers released from the hard labour of the mills. She would be waiting to feed the milkman's horse in the morning, and must have felt sorry for them as they pulled the tram she was sitting in. On a summer evening the organ-grinder would have come, with little birds to sell. She would want him to open the cage, to let them fly to fields where the suburbs hadn't yet reached.

They moved to Broughty Ferry, where Mrs Begbie's mother became district nurse. Mrs Begbie went to training college in Edinburgh, and was to teach in Wallacetown Primary for ten years. William McGonagall was still scribbling when she was in her early twenties. Did he sell her a broadsheet with one of his awful odes? She must have seen the *Discovery* launched into "the silvery Tay" in 1901. Did her relatives know the wee man from Kirriemuir who sent Peter Pan flying into the world in 1904?

That was the time of the Sunday promenades, the ladies in their long skirts and elaborate hats, the men in bowlers. The city's footballers were in long shorts, and bairns went barefoot in the wynds. You could take a pleasure steamer to Perth.

Mrs Begbie married in 1910. Her husband was in Customs & Excise, Dundee. It's discourteous to work out a lady's age as she approaches the mature years, but Mrs Begbie would have seen the Black Watch, the city's regiment, going off to war. Many didn't make it back. She would have also seen the unemployed who were in danger of becoming permanent fixtures at street corners in the hopeless thirties.

But Dundee has changed so much since Mrs Begbie's younger days. William Adam provided a most gracious Town House as a replacement for the sixteenth century Tolbooth. The Town House stood on the south side of the High Street but was brought down in the name of modernisation. As for the Caledonian Station. . .

A fourth monarch was crowned in Mrs. Begbie's lifetime and one abdicated. Then she started getting royal telegrams, and at the last count had twelve. Having lived all her life in Broughty Ferry, Mrs Begbie has been most comfortable in Dundee's Pine Grove Home since 1973. This face is as stalwart as the city it has watched for over a hundred years.

Little Charles looks apprehensive as his parents, Lieutenant and Mrs Leighton of Perthshire compose him for the chaplain. The baby is being christened on board HMS *Unicorn,* the oldest British built warship afloat. Launched in 1824, the 1084 ton frigate carried 46 guns and had a crew of 334. It was towed to Dundee in 1873 and became a training ship. It can be visited at Victoria Dock. Other vessels have carried that illustrious name. The bell which looks big enough to bath Charles in came from the fifteenth and last *Unicorn* built for the Royal Navy, the aircraft carrier launched in 1939. A benevolent braided "godfather" smiles as he witnesses the little midshipman getting a wet head.

Dundee technology is helping to keep distant Nigeria on the move.
Dunclare Dispensers of Wester Gourdie Estate manufacture forecourt
dispensing equipment. Founded in 1983 and flourishing, they took
their name from Dun (for Dundee) and Clare, the managing director's
daughter.

Dundee born and dedicated: James McIntosh Patrick in his waterfront studio at his 80th birthday in 1987, his window a still-life of the Tay railway bridge. Lauded as one of Scotland's finest landscape artists of this century, he has been out in the Angus countryside in all weathers, even using a stove to keep his paints malleable.

Alan Lowden, who runs Invergowrie post office with his wife, talks to his grandson Nicky. This village four miles from Dundee on the Perthshire-Angus boundary claims to be the place where the first Christian church was erected in Scotland north of the Tay. Who can now find the site of Cater Milly, a Roman camp which dated to Agricola's eighth campaign? Another campaign in the nineteen sixties failed to save Bullionfield. It was a meal mill in the early eighteenth century, then turned to flax scutching before converting to a waulk-mill. At its closure it was making paper. The post office is in one of the oldest buildings in this village, and maybe Nicky will be behind its counter one day.

The junior is not having his name taken for foul play. The date is 28 November 1987, and Dundee United are about to play Dundee. Jim McLean, United Manager, is having a good luck word with Marc Henry from Alyth, the mascot for that game. Football began in the city over a century ago, with St Clements the first club to achieve prominence. Dundee Harp drew its players from the large Irish pool in the jute mills, kicking a ball the ideal way to exercise cramped muscles. In March 1909 Pat Reilly, a successful city cycle maker and dealer, helped to found Dundee Hibernian. (There are no free tickets for guessing that the jersey was emerald green). In 1923 Dundee Hibernian became Dundee United. The city erupted on 14 May 1983 when Dundee United beat Dundee to win the Scottish League Championship for the first time. Jim McLean, who became Manager in 1971, has always looked to the younger generation for future players. Marc's mother says: "from reports from his dad and the man who takes Cub football, Marc's a good player." Maybe he'll make the Tannadice squad.

These fans are a credit to Dundee. The photograph was taken on 20th May 1987 when United played Gothenburg at Tannadice in the second leg of the UEFA cup final. It was the only time the UEFA cup contest had been staged in Scotland, because no other team has reached the final. Though it was a 1-1 draw, United lost 2-1 on aggregate. A couple of thousand United fans had gone out to the first leg in Gothenburg. A fortnight later when Gothenburg came to Tannadice, an international television audience watched the United fans cheering the Swedes, though their own team was being beaten overall. FIFA was so impressed by their behaviour in Sweden, but particularly in Dundee, that they gave the United supporters FIFA's first "fair play" award.

REDISCOVERY

It took Captain Scott's ship 85 years to make it home, having been laid up in ice, followed by major alterations, then a long docking in London. Dundonians are unanimous: the wait has been worth it.

A quartet of Dundee whalers had explored the potential of the South Atlantic and the Antarctic region in 1892. In 1901 the National Antarctic Expedition appointed a naval officer, Robert Scott as the commander. Since no suitable ship could be found, one had to be built. Because of the city's expertise in building whalers, the £51,000 contract went to the Dundee Shipbuilders' Company Ltd. The specifications called for timber construction to withstand ice pressure and also to make the ship non-magnetic.

Discovery was already an illustrious name in exploration. In 1875-76 a Dundee whaler had sailed on an expedition to the North Pole. Its design was enlarged and modified for the 1901 vessel. The new *Discovery* (probably the sixth ship to bear the name) was 226 feet long, barque rigged, its sails supplied by Baxter Bros., that famous city mill. Gourlay Bros., provided the powerful steam engine.

The watertight holds had to take two years' provisions, and insulation had to be thick. Coal was precious, since the ship needed up to six tons daily. The ingenuity of design allowed the bronze propeller and the wood and steel rudder to be raised through the hull when in danger of damage from thick ice.

A bottle of Australian wine sent *Discovery* out into the Tay estuary in March 1901. That July it left London Docks. Scott soon saw the drawbacks: the under-canvassed ship was slow, and the masts should have been put further forward. Also, it rolled heavily. An elusive intake of water was christened the "Dundee Leak."

Nevertheless, Scott surveyed 500 miles of the great ice barrier and discovered King Edward VII Land before returning to McMurdo Sound for the winter. But Shackleton had to be evacuated through scurvy, and *Discovery* had to sit out two winters in the ice. Explosives eventually had to be used to free the ship, which arrived back in England in September 1904. It was the closest expedition to the South Pole.

After an extensive refit in 1923-24, *Discovery* sailed again as a research ship concerned with preserving whales from extinction through overfishing. In 1931 *Discovery* was laid up in East India Dock, London. Sea Scouts, then the Admiralty, used the ship for training. In 1979 it was opened as part of the Historic Ship Collection in St Katherine's Dock, London.

But it is really a Dundee boat, and it came home to a massive welcome. Now in Victoria Dock, close to where she was built, *Discovery* is being restored to the 1924 refit. But it will still be possible to stand on the deck and imaginatively set out again with Scott on that 1901 voyage to the land of ice.

Lifelike models on board *Discovery*: Captain Scott (left) and Dr Wilson (right) on their polar trek, and below, the ship locked in the ice of McMurdo Sound.

Look left, to where these rails run by the Tay. Part of it is reclaimed land, a city determined to go places.

Since you'll never guess what these rollers are, they're takers-in, used for carding cotton, and are manufactured in the waterfront works of Wm. R. Stewart & Sons, the biggest and best independent hacklemakers left in the world. Hacklemaking grew out of the traditional trade of producing combs for flax processing and developed into the manufacture of all types of pinned combs and rollers for textile working. As the jute industry declined in Dundee, this enterprising firm set out to follow the markets in the Far East. They now export to 56 countries. Their office at Marine Parade was part of the shipyard that built the *Discovery*, now moored nearby in Victoria Dock. Mr. Roderick Stewart is a trustee of the Dundee Heritage Trust which looks after Captain Scott's ship, and both he and his father Captain Rennie Stewart are governors of the Unicorn Trust. That historic vessel is moored outside their door.

A JAMMY STORY

Great addictions have accidental beginnings. In 1797 John Keiller, a small-time Dundee grocer, bought a cargo of bitter Seville oranges from a ship seeking shelter from a storm. His wife Janet, already adept at making quince jam, decided to boil the oranges with sugar. Thus marmalade bubbled into life by the Tay estuary. Having tried it out among family and friends, the Keillers sold it in their shop. When it went down a treat in Dundee John Keiller decided to sell his grocery business and concentrate on marketing marmalade.

The firm of James Keiller & Son Ltd was founded in 1797. Their marmalade travelled over the globe in the distinctive white pot (still produced today) and was spread on bread in the middle of blizzards and in heatwaves. But when punitive import duties on sugar threatened the continuing prosperity of the Dundee firm in 1846 the canny Keillers established a factory on Guernsey, where sugar was imported duty-free.

In 1874 with the removal of sugar duty the Guernsey advantage went, and that factory was transferred to Silvertown in London's east end. Fires in 1860 and 1900 did much damage to the Dundee factory, and to Silvertown in 1899. By this time Keiller were also substantial producers of confectionery and chocolate.

The London factory was lost in the Blitz, and though it was rebuilt, the company decided that further expansion of manufacturing facilities would be concentrated in Dundee. After the war a new preserves factory was built in Mains Loan, the site of today's preserves and confectionery production. Another Mains Loan factory was built for the manufacture of the Swiss chocolate Toblerone for exclusive distribution in the UK.

But other firms wanted to get their teeth into these Tayside goodies, and in 1951 Keiller were acquired by Crosse & Blackwell Ltd. Ten years later, when Crosse & Blackwell were themselves taken over, Keiller became part of Nestle, the Swiss multi-national. But the mixed marriage was not a success, and in the nineteen seventies Keiller sales declined alarmingly, with heavy trading losses. In 1981 Nestle announced the closure of the company.

Then the Okhai family, originally from Malawi, came in before the production line was stopped for the last time. Their success story had begun with the export of vacuum flasks. Okhai put jars of Keiller marmalade back on breakfast tables before the Bury based confectionery manufacturer Barker & Dobson took over in 1986. The Dundee factory is now one of the most modern marmalade and confectionery production units in Europe.

Royalty knows what is tasteful. In 1914 King George V and Queen Mary visited Keiller. In 1955 the Queen and Duke of Edinburgh toured the Mains Loan plant, and in 1983 the Princess of Wales came to charm everyone. The bi-centenary of the company will be in 1997, when you'll still be able to sample Janet's original idea — if the shop's not sold out.

Son of the Provost, local boy Adam Duncan enlisted in the navy in
1746. By 1796 he was an Admiral, and the following year showed his
strategic brilliance by defeating the Dutch fleet· at the battle of
Camperdown. He took the title first Viscount Camperdown, and his
son had William Burn build a befitting mansion in 1824. One of
Scotland's finest country houses, its stained glass dome is its dazzling
glory. Lady Camperdown apparently liked to wander solitary as a
cloud, because the arrangement of the rooms kept servants and
guests out of her way. Today, Dundonians can dine in the restaurant
while children who want to follow Adam Duncan to sea can restage the
battle of Camperdown with large model ships in the huge park.

It isn't a herd of deer that has come down from the Angus hills in search of sustenance in the city, but a set of cold cast resin sculptures by David Annand in Dundee Technology Park, part of the enterprising Dundee Public Arts Programme. This has grown out of the project Public Art in Blackness 1982-85, an area left derelict and depressed through the decline in the textile industry. Mosaics and standing sculptures have made Blackness more attractive to new businesses as well as old residents. Now the entire city has been surveyed, and artworks will be appearing elsewhere. The Public Arts Programme, which is backed by the Scottish Arts Council and the Scottish Development Agency, works closely with industry, which is why these deer are leaping out of the Technology Park at the western gateway to a city many companies are discovering. David Annand's deer received the Royal Society of British Sculptors' Owto Biet award for the best sculpture outside London in 1987.

From the administrative centre of Tayside House the camera looks down busy Reform Street to the pillared façade of the High School of Dundee, appropriately sited in Euclid Crescent. The history of this place of learning is the history of the nation itself. In 1239 the Abbot of Lindores was instructed to build a grammar school in the new burgh of Dundee. Blind Harry the ballad-maker tells us that William Wallace was a pupil. Once grant-aided, the school is now private. The present buildings date from the eighteen thirties.

The billboard comment could also apply to the architectural styles of this quarter of Dundee.

There are ways other than by bridge to travel to and from Dundee. The airport was opened in 1966 and offers scheduled services to Manchester, Aberdeen, Carlisle and London. But that is only a small part of its activity. There is a flying club, and air taxis coming and going. Business Air's first international scheduled flight to Espjerg, Denmark, took off in April 1988. This airport by the estuary is going places.

A stately horseshoe staircase leads to the Albert Institute, now the McManus Galleries, memorial to Queen Victoria's beloved consort. Dundee hadn't the cash in its coffers to afford it, so the Baxters and other potentates called for their cheque-books as they were to do so often. The great Sir George Gilbert Scott, architect of Glasgow University, did Dundee proud through his adaptation of a design destined for Hamburg, but never realised in stone; fitting, considering Prince Albert's nationality. But the way into the Galleries is at the other end, at ground level.

DUNDEE TREASURES ON DISPLAY

It was Dr Patrick Blair who founded the city's first museum, the "Hall of Rarities" and "Physik Garden" at the beginning of the eighteenth century. Then in 1824 the Watt Institution was established, named after the famous steam engineer. Working men were educated in the building in Constitution Road (now the YMCA) which also mounted exhibitions. But the foundation of the Albert Institute was the real beginning of a museum service fit for Dundee.

But the Institute proved too small to hold a museum and art gallery as well as a library, and had to be extended twice within twenty years of its opening in 1867. When the Central Library was removed to the splendid new Wellgate Centre in 1978, it was an opportunity to give more space to the museum and galleries through a major redevelopment programme.

The Albert Institute has now been renamed the McManus Galleries in honour of a former Lord Provost, and there are days of pleasure and education for the Dundonian and the visitor within its elegant walls. Three major galleries are devoted to the following themes: the history of Dundee and its environs, archaeology, trade and industry, social and civic history.

Royal visits are remembered. Queen Victoria's trip to Dundee in 1844 was the first by a reigning monarch for almost 200 years. In 1933 the Prince of Wales was in the city to look at public works projects organised for the relief of unemployment, and the camera was there to capture his concern.

The reconstructed trade premises in the Galleries will bring back wistful memories of days when inflation meant pumping up a bicycle tyre, a straw basket on the handlebars for the messages. None of your frozen stuffs and check-out queues: the grocer in his long white apron offers Best Treacle, butter patted between boards. There is a rack of boxes of Crawfords Delightful Biscuits which many a mother, worried about how little was left in her purse, was only too glad to buy broken.

Stop at the pub, with its ivory-handled pumps that required pulling power, not a gas cylinder. There are shelves of old dark bottles of beer. But next door you may wish to avert your eyes as a young lady from one of the grander houses in the city (maybe a jute baron's niece?) is about to step into her hip-bath that took half a dozen kettles to fill. Her fresh white linen is laid out, her silver dressing-set is on the marble wash-stand. You can ogle her, but you can also learn something: public baths were established in the eighteen forties in Dundee, and, for a touch of exotica for tired mill-toilers, there were Turkish Baths too.

The shawled model sits at the grate in the tenement kitchen, showing how hard it was to feed them when it wasn't a matter of pulling a switch. But one place you want to avoid is the small hinged door with the spying-hole from the condemned cell in Dundee Tolbooth.

Though Mary Slessor was born in Aberdeen in 1848, at the age of ten she moved with her family to Dundee, and is therefore considered to be one of the city's most cherished daughters. She was a "half-timer" in Baxter's works, meaning that half her day went to flax working, and the remainder to learning in the mill school. After training in Edinburgh she went out to Calabar in West Africa in 1876. Loved both as a missionary and a civil magistrate, Mary's selfless life is remembered in a memorial window in the Galleries. Her 1911 diary and her compass used in Calabar are on show, but it was her heart that told her the true direction to take in life.

One of the most successful reconstructions is that of the dwelling made of branches as it would have looked at Douglasmuir Settlement in the Lunan Valley 2,500 years ago. An eerie figure squats by the fire, and the sound effects of domestic animals are enough to convince you that you're in a farmyard.

Upstairs Dundee's collection of paintings and artefacts can stand comparison with any in the country. One of the treasures is the Scrymgeour Gold Snuff Mull, made in Scotland about 1725. No other Scottish gold snuff mull of this period is known. It's a unique acquisition of national importance and local significance (since the Scrymgeours were at Dudhope Castle) purchased by the Galleries in 1986.

The silversmithing skills of Dundee are represented by the display of Scottish provincial silver in the applied art collection. Genteel Dundonians poured from Alexander Johnstone's silver bullet teapot in the mid eighteenth century, when that precious leaf had to be locked away. How many Jacobite pamphlets were perused by the light of John Steven's pair of silver candlesticks, made in Dundee in 1740? Long-cased Dundee clocks under which senior citizens of another century dozed continue to tick on in the Galleries. The city as a shipping port is symbolised by the world's oldest mariner's astrolabe, made in Portugal in 1555 by Lopo Homem.

The McManus's collection of European and British painting is wide-ranging, with the Scottish representation strong. Dundee has had distinguished artists such as George Dutch Davidson (1879-1901) and John Duncan (1866-1945). That masterly exponent James McIntosh Patrick, chronicler of his native city and its environs and still wielding the brush at over 80, has his rightful place here. Though it is Broughty Ferry's lamented loss, the transfer of the Orchar Collection to Dundee is to the city's benefit.

But there are other museums as well. Hard by the Howff is Barrack Street Natural History Museum, its dramatic highlight the skeleton of the male humpbacked whale harpooned in the Tay in 1883. Originally a library and gallery built in 1910 through the munificence of Andrew Carnegie, Barrack Street Museum is being re-developed as Dundee's Natural History Museum. Watch out for displays of urban as well as rural wildlife, for foxes are moving into the City of Discovery and have ways of opening black plastic sacks.

It takes a little study to see that the painting beyond the gentleman with the catalogue in the McManus Galleries is of Highland cattle in a swirling mountain mist. The artist, Peter Graham (1836-1921) was immensely popular in his day.

A quartet of models from the McManus Galleries' reconstruction of past life in Dundee, when a sixpence went such a long way.

HILLTOWN

Hilltown was well placed, the road north and east from the walled town of Dundee. It was called the Mains Road, and in the fullness of time facing cottages on either side of this route formed a street or "Hilltown." Other dwellings were built behind. It was a countryside of corn and bleaching greens, of contented cows, of spinners sitting singing in their booths.

The Hilltown of Dudhope also went by the name of the Rotten Row, but had its name and status elevated into a "Burgh of Barony" in 1643 by a charter from Charles I in favour of Sir James Scrymgeour, twelfth Constable of Dundee and second Viscount Dudhope.

A visitor to Hilltown in 1776 recorded: "It is vastly lightsome, having a fore view, it lying so high, and the inhabitants have as much fresh air as if they were a number of miles in the country."

Hilltown claims an unannounced royal visit in the early sixteenth century, as James V wandered in disguise, anxious to see for himself how safe and happy his subjects were. He took the Mains Road up through the Baronie, and met up with Coutie a drover from Dundee.

They were set upon by a band of robbers, and the drover's dog put up the most spirited defence. But they were outnumbered, and the disguised monarch shouted out: "Feight on, Cowtie, the face of a King is terrible!" Realising who they were fighting, and thinking that reinforcements were about to arrive, the villains fled. For his defence of his king the drover was given his own wynd, which became known as Cowtie's Wynd.

Hilltown was a rough place in these times, as witness the "spiked maiden" torture iron in Dudhope Castle, and the Tolbooth in which the Baron Courts were held, where the placing of a lighted candle on the table, and the judge's verdict sealed in a sheet of paper spelt doom to the guilty.

But Hilltown was also a happy place of many trades. The dwellings had long rigs which became the courts and wynds where crafts were carried out. In the middle of the eighteenth century the cottages were thatched, the bonnet-makers so numerous that the Baronie was sometimes referred to in official documents as "Bonat Raw."

There they sat, in the shelter of their cottages, gossiping and knitting, the blue bonnets taking shape on their needles. Yankees swaggered about in Hilltown cloth when Indians still had their ancestral lands. (Hilltown didn't make feathered headdresses). Flat fish were sold at the Skate Market by the men while the women went round the doors hawking partans and whelks. When the Town Hangman had too much time on his hands he acted as Scavenger, swine roaming the street his perk.

Hilltown had fairs and funerals, and queer customs like the bridegroom getting treacle and ink rubbed into his feet. When the Rotten Row cottages were crushed by the tenements, a lot more than the skill of thatching was lost.

Elderly Hilltowners use the street for chatting, the young for football against the backdrop of the Derby Street multis, said to be "nearly as tall as the top of the Law" when they were completed in 1971. But they retain historical connections through their names, Bucklemaker and Butterburn Courts. Bucklemaker Wynd, which housed a branch of the Hammermen, is now part of Victoria Road. Butterburn, at the top of Hilltown, was a rivulet which rose in the Law and flowed down what is now Hill Street.

The clock is a distinctive Hilltown landmark, a meeting point. Is the gentleman trying to read the inscription? It says: "presented to the community of Dundee by Charles Barrie, one of the representatives of the seventh ward, December 1900." It's a pity that today's councillors don't leave such useful monuments.

When the last number's been called, someone has to do the sweeping-up. Blackness Hall was part of old St Joseph's School whose gates still stand, displaying the papal coat of arms. The hall became a vital centre for the community, and many Dundonians who are resting their feet now can remember wartime dances. The hall was sold to a development company several years ago and, who knows, might become a gathering place again, though the footwork will be different this time.

Ally Bally is on the air again, entertaining Tayside, Angus and North-East Fife listeners mid morning, Monday to Friday with records, chat, news. Radio Tay your friendly station began to make itself heard in 1980. Though now a wholly owned subsidiary of Radio Forth, it retains its individuality, its appeal. Ally is Presentation Controller and Head of Music.

The electric light you are studying this photograph by may be coming courtesy of this technician. N.I. Transformers of East Kingsway make power transformers for distributing electricity from generating stations, through the lines to factories and houses. This is their jubilee year, and their product is helping to "transform" faraway places like Burma.

The name of the short film Grampian Television is shooting is surely Courage, and the two stars are a man and a dog. John Dearie from Glasgow needs a very special friend because he is a deaf-mute as well as being blind. Rikki from Forfar Guide-Dog Centre waits patiently at the kerb. Broughty Ferry is apparently an excellent place for training because of the grid lay-out of the streets. Since John cannot speak to Rikki, every touch of his hand carries a message, including a special one for "good boy." In addition an acoustic monitor strapped to John's wrist gives traffic vibrations. In the middle Ron Thompson, senior reporter, provides the touching commentary.

In 1564, during a visit to Dundee with Lord Darnley, Mary Queen of Scots gave the Howff to the lieges as a resting place. Where Grey Friars once gathered fallen fruit, "godlie, honest and vertuous" townsfolk are interred. For two centuries until 1776 Dundee Incorporated Trades congregated in the Howff, holding their meetings by the graves of members: an investment in the world to come? Burial was discontinued here in 1857. A girl roller-skates past the shadowed grid of the open gate, an invitation to office-workers to stroll through this quiet city centre spot at lunchtime. Deciphering inscriptions under the gnarled trees is a change from staring at computer screens in this age of technological trade, and an ancestor could be discovered. It is claimed that the Howff's collection of funerary monuments is "of a quality second only to Greyfriars Kirk in Edinburgh."

Bonar Carelle are a brand new company, a worthy successor to jute. The factory on the Wester Gourdie Estate was opened by the Queen and Duke of Edinburgh in the summer of 1987. They manufacture a range of non-woven fabrics using "powder bonding" technique, developed in the USA by their sister company in conjunction with Eastman Kodak. A field leader, Bonar Carelle's products have a wide and vital application, including gowns for hospital operating theatres.

It would be a foolish man who would confuse Dundee and Dundee United, especially in the home city they share. This photograph shows manager Jocky Scott with (left to right): Thomas Coyne, Stuart Rafferty and Thomas McKinley. A history of the club is in preparation, so here's a preview. Towards the end of last century a local club called the "East End" had gone to great effort and expense to bring its ground, Carolina Port, up to a standard comparable with anywhere in Scotland. In 1893 the "East End" and another local club, "Our Boys", amalgamated, and, as Dundee Football Club was admitted into the Scottish League First Division. The new club may have got off the ground, but had literally to get off its ground, Carolina Port, when the lease was given to Strathmore, another club. West Craigie Park became Dundee Football Club's ground, but the club ran into such serious financial difficulties that in 1898 it had to go into liquidation. However, a new organising committee came into force, and a new ground, Dens Park was secured. The rest, as they say is history, but harmonious history, since the rivalry between Dundee and Dundee United has always been in good spirit. Praising Jocky Scott's managerial drive, the club historian writes: "There is a regular growth in the number of supporters' clubs springing up all round the country and the Junior Dark Blues, for the very young, keep going from strength to strength."

116

There are no skyscrapers in Dundee, so in the interests of the panoramic view the photographer had to take to the air. Bottom (right) is regional headquarters Tayside House, with its walkway to the Swimming and Leisure Centre. (This isn't so that harassed officials can cool off). Beside the complicated geometry of the roundabout is the curving elegance of Whitehall Crescent (1885-89). History, however haphazard, has had to give way to the combustion engine. Last century this area was a dark warren of courts and passages, "receptacles of filth." The only transfer its tenants could look forward to was to the nearby Howff cemetery.

The nurses perambulate a baby in Dudhope Park, adjacent to the Royal Infirmary, built in neo-Elizabethan style by two London architects in the eighteen fifties. The old infirmary was visited by epidemics caused by poor social provision such as contaminated drinking water. In 1847-48 typhus, smallpox and other scourges carried off 299 patients. But only seven years later, on completion of the new Infirmary, the Building Chronicle commented: "now that the building is finished the Directors are at a loss what to do with it, the unusually healthy condition of the town and the enormously expensive accommodation being rather striking. It is accordingly being offered to the government as a hospital for sick and wounded soldiers." The Infirmary is still in use, with laughter the best way of getting well, as witness this girl in the children's ward. The next bed has "support" sitting on it as well as hanging from the rail above. Ninewells, Dundee's mega-hospital, completed in 1975, was the first entirely new teaching hospital built in Britain and is still a leader in care and equipment, which local generosity helps to provide.

What is a Roman soldier doing in Monifieth? The answer has been
hard to come by, but is nothing to do with Agricola's victory over the
Caledonii at Mons Graupius, thought to be near Stonehaven. This is
the memorial to the 1914-18 war erected by the town council to some
disquiet, since a contemporary soldier would have been more fitting.
Economics appear to have dictated design, but now it looks costly,
pleasingly classical. Each time he passes it, ex Provost Alexander
Cameron Watt lifts his hat. His father died from wounds in the First
War, and his brother's name is on the 1939-45 panel.